The State Flags of our Nation

THOMAS PUBLICATIONS
Gettysburg, PA 17325

INTRODUCTION

The United States of America is one of the youngest nations in the world (at a little over 200 years old) and also one of the largest, richest, and most powerful. The United States grew out of thirteen British colonies that banded together in protest of the restraints and taxes imposed on them by the royal government. The American Revolution began in 1775, and July 4, 1776, the day the Declaration of Independence was signed, is celebrated as the nation's birthday. The colonies, led by great men such as Thomas Jefferson, Benjamin Franklin, Patrick Henry, and George Washington, organized their own government based on principles of democracy and individual freedom.

In the years since 1776, the United States has grown from thirteen small states along the eastern border of North America to fifty states encompassing the width of North America, from the Atlantic to the Pacific, and including land near the North Pole and in the Pacific Ocean. And symbolizing the traditions and heritage of each of these fifty states is a state flag.

Citizens often see the flag of their state flying over government buildings, in state parks, and other important places. Yet few people are sure why their state flag looks the way it does. In *The State Flags of Our Nation*, each of the fifty state flags is presented in full color, along with a short history of the state and a description of its flag.

Traditionally, the use of flags can be traced back thousands of years, to the earliest hunters and warriors who used crude signs made of animal skins, furs, and feathers to help them to identify friend or foe. These early flags were carried on the end of a pole and waved about so that everyone could see which tribe they belonged to. Over time, flags have evolved into more complex, colorful, and intricately-patterned banners, but their meaning has remained the same. A flag is a symbol—and the people who carry or display that symbol belong to a certain group or country.

In the Middle Ages, the different parts of flags were given names based on the rules of heraldry. The whole cloth, or background, of the flag is called the *field,* or **ground.** The rectangle found in the upper left-hand corner of many flags is called the **canton.** Each of these areas can contain designs or colors that symbolize something important to the group represented by that flag. For example, the flag of the United States has a field of thirteen red and white stripes, which represent the thirteen original colonies. Its canton contains fifty white stars, representing all fifty states in the Union, on a blue background.

Each of the fifty United States has its own flag. They represent the unique features of each individual state which makes up our great nation. A few states were once independent countries for brief periods, and had their own national flags. These national flags evolved into their state flags. One example is California; its state flag is white with a brown bear—the grizzly. Texas flies a flag with a single star, representing the "Lone Star State." Regardless of how a state flag came to be, it is flown with pride, together with the "Stars and Stripes" of the United States.

Sarah C. Rodgers
Thomas Publications
Gettysburg, PA

ALABAMA

The Heart of Dixie

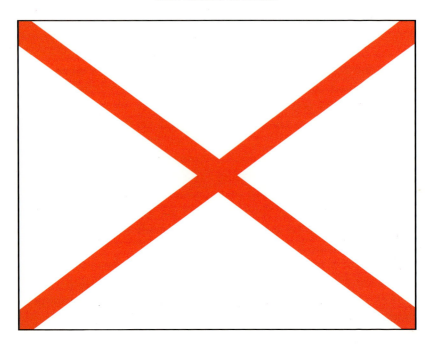

The Alabama state flag has a crimson cross of St. Andrew on a white field. This flag is the only state flag that is exactly square. The flag is based upon the Confederate Battle flag.

1540 Explored by Hernando de Soto for Spain
1702 Permanently settled by the French
1819 Admitted to the Union as the 22nd state

Capital—Montgomery

Although the French settled Alabama, they ceded it to England after the French and Indian War. In 1783, England ceded the southern part to Spain, but in 1795 most of the area was claimed by the United States. Spain finally relinquished its claims and a separate Alabama Territory was organized in 1817. Two years later, a constitution was drafted and Alabama became a state.

ALASKA

Land of the Midnight Sun

This flag was designed by a thirteen year old seventh grader named Benny Benson. His design won a state contest in 1927. The blue in the flag is for the state flower (forget-me-not) and the Alaskan sky. The gold is for the natural wealth. The North Star is symbolic of Alaska's position in relation to the heavens, and the Big Dipper represents the Great Bear, or strength.

1741 Explored by Vitus Bering for Russia
1784 Permanently settled by Russian fur traders
1959 Admitted to the Union as the 49th state

Capital—Juneau

The Russians were the first to settle Alaska, and maintained control of the region until the late 19th century, despite Spanish, French, and British claims. When Great Britain threatened to seize the area in 1867, Russia sold Alaska to the United States. The state was created from the Alaska Territory, organized in 1912.

ARIZONA

Grand Canyon State

The Arizona state flag has a copper star, symbolizing Arizona's most important mineral, rising from a field of blue into the rays of a setting sun, which represents it as a western state. The 13 rays stand for the original states of the Union. Blue and gold are Arizona's colors, and the dark blue also stands for loyalty to the United States.

1539 Explored by Marcos de Niza for Spain
1752 Permanently settled by the Spanish
1912 Admitted to the Union as the 48th state

Capital—Phoenix

Spanish Jesuits organized missions in the area after 1690, but no settlements were established until 1752. When Mexico won its independence from Spain in 1821, the area was organized as the Mexican Territory of New Mexico. It was annexed by the United States at the end of the Mexican War in 1848. The state was formed from the Arizona Territory, organized in 1863.

6

ARKANSAS

The Land of Opportunity

The Arkansas state flag has a large white diamond on a red field bordered in blue, with 25 white stars, representing its status as the 25th state. The blue star above the name shows that it belonged to the Confederacy. The other three blue stars represent France, Spain, and the United States, nations which have owned the land, and also that Arkansas was the third state created from the Louisiana Purchase.

1541 Explored by Hernando de Soto for Spain
1686 Permanently settled by the French
1836 Admitted to the Union as the 25th state

Capital—Little Rock

In 1763, Jacques Marquette and Louis Joliet visited the Arkansas region. After La Salle claimed it for France in 1682, French colonization began. Although France ceded the area to Spain after the French and Indian War, Spain returned it to France in 1801. In 1803, France sold the Territory of Arkansas as part of the Louisiana Purchase. The Territory adopted a constitution in 1836 and statehood was granted.

7

CALIFORNIA

The Golden State

CALIFORNIA REPUBLIC

The California state flag is called the Bear Flag, for the grizzly bear, a symbol of independence. The lone star and the words "California Republic" show that California was not part of the Union when the flag was first used by settlers in the revolt against Mexico in 1846.

1542   Explored by Juan Rodriguez Cabrillo and Bartolome Ferrelo for Spain
1769   Permanently settled by Spanish missionaries
1850   Admitted to the Union as the 31st state

Capital—Sacramento

California became a territory of Mexico in 1825 after Mexican independence. American settlers quickly moved into the area and, in 1846, rebelled against the Mexican government. In an 1848 treaty, the United States annexed California. Settlers flocked to the area during the 1849 gold rush. Before the area could be organized as a territory, residents drew up a state constitution and elected a governor and legislature.

COLORADO

Centennial State

The Colorado state flag has three stripes- blue, white, and blue- representing the blue sky and white snow-capped mountains. The letter C stands for Colorado, and the golden disk inside represents gold, the early source of mineral wealth.

1540 Explored by Francisco Vasquez Coronado for Spain
1858 Permanently settled by American fur traders and miners
1876 Admitted to the Union as the 38th state

Capital—Denver

Although the region was explored first by the Spanish and later by Americans, few attempts were made to colonize it until the mid-nineteenth century. Sold to the United States as part of the Louisiana Purchase, a portion of the area was claimed by Mexico until after the Mexican War in 1848. The state was formed from the Colorado Territory, organized in 1861 after the discovery of gold in the region.

CONNECTICUT

The Constitution State

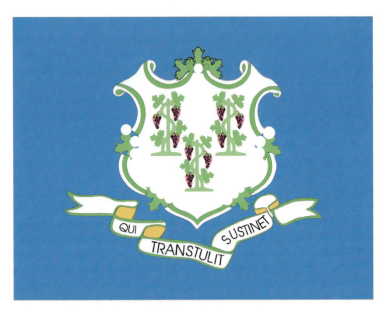

The Connecticut state flag is azure blue, with three grapevines resting on a silver-white shield in the center of the flag. The grapevines are thought to represent the three settlements (New Haven, Saybrook and Connecticut) which formed the state. Beneath the shield, on a white streamer, is the state motto, which means "He who brought us over will sustain us."

One of the thirteen original colonies
1614   Explored by Adriaen Block for the Dutch
1634-5 Permanently settled by the English
1788   Admitted to the Union as the 5th state

Capital—Hartford

Dutch residents from New Amsterdam established a trading post near present day Hartford in 1633, but it was the English from the Massachusetts Bay Colony who made the initial move to colonize the area. In 1638-39, the Fundamental Orders of Connecticut were adopted, a document that gave more governmental power to the people.

10

DELAWARE

The First State

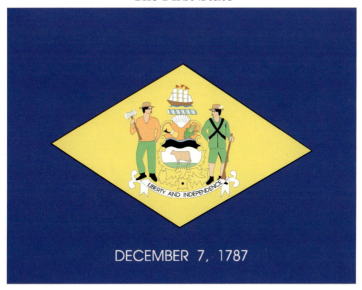

The Delaware state flag has a buff-colored diamond on a background of colonial blue, with the state coat of arms on the diamond. The date on the flag, December 7, 1787, is the date Delaware ratified the Constitution. The diamond represents an earlier nickname, the Diamond State. The coat of arms symbolizes the occupations of the state's early days, shipping, farming, and hunting.

One of the thirteen original colonies
1609 Explored by Henry Hudson for the Dutch
1638 Permanently settled by the Swedes
1787 Admitted to the Union as the 1st state

Capital—Dover

Peter Minuit established the first successful settlement with the New Sweden Company at Fort Christina (Wilmington). Fighting began in 1655 between the Dutch and the Swedes in the area, and the Dutch prevailed. When the English drove them from New Netherland in 1664, Delaware became a part of New York. In 1682, it was included as a part of William Penn's royal grant. In 1704, Delaware split from Pennsylvania and became a separate colony.

FLORIDA

The Sunshine State

The Florida state flag has the state seal in the center on a white field. The red diagonal cross was inspired by the battle flag of the Confederate States of America, to which Florida belonged. The Indian woman represents Florida's first inhabitants, the Seminoles. The seal also represents the diversity of the state, the land of sunshine, flowers, palm trees, rivers and lakes. The state motto "In God We Trust" is prominent on the flag.

1513 Explored by Ponce de Leon for Spain
1565 Permanently settled by the Spanish
1845 Admitted to the Union as the 27th state

Capital—Tallahassee

The first permanent European settlement in America was established by the Spanish in 1565 at St. Augustine. In 1763, Britain received Florida in a trade for Havana but receded it to Spain twenty years later. In 1819, the United States acquired Florida from Spain and organized it as a territory in 1822.

GEORGIA

The Peach State

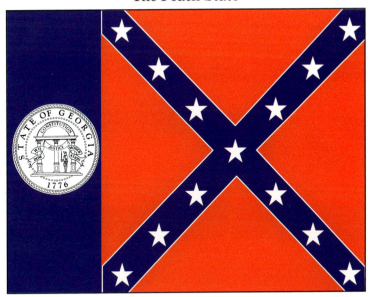

The Georgia state flag has two parts: One is a vertical blue band with the state seal, and the other depicts the battle flag of the Confederacy. The date 1776 is the date of the Declaration of Independence. The arch, representing the Constitution, is supported by three pillars and is symbolic of how the three branches of government support the Constitution.

Last of the thirteen original colonies
1540   Explored by Hernando de Soto for Spain
1733   Permanently settled by the English
1788   Admitted to the Union as the 4th state

Capital—Atlanta

Pedro Menendez de Aviles attempted a coastal Spanish settlement in 1565. England claimed the territory in the 17th century, but did not colonize it until the 18th century. In 1732 George II granted a charter to a board of trustees, including James Oglethorpe, who wanted to establish a colony for impoverished Englishmen and religious refugees. In 1753, the trustees gave up their charter and Georgia became a royal colony.

HAWAII

The Aloha State

The Hawaii state flag has eight horizontal stripes, alternately white, red, and blue, which represent the eight main islands. The British Union Jack in the upper left corner dates to the 1790s when British explorers gave Hawaii's king a British flag.

1778 Explored by James Cook for England
1820 Permanently settled by American missionaries
1959 Admitted to the Union as the 50th state

Capital—Honolulu

After James Cook first visited the islands in 1778, they were frequented by traders. As American missionaries arrived, Hawaiians were converted to Christianity, and businesses were founded in the sugar and pineapple trade. United States recognition came in 1842, followed by reciprocal trade agreements, the creation of a republic, and eventual annexation in 1898. The state was formed from the Territory of Hawaii, organized in 1900.

14

IDAHO

The Gem State

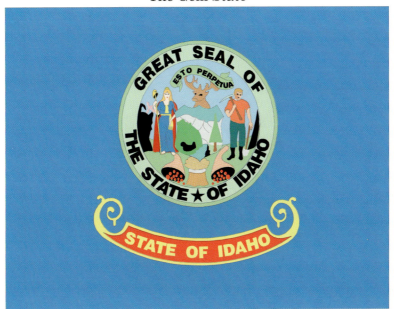

The Idaho state flag has the state seal in color, centered on a blue field. The words "State of Idaho" appear on a red streamer beneath the seal. On the seal, the woman represents liberty, justice and equality. The man is a miner. The pictures represent the main industries of forestry, farming and mining. The cornucopias are symbols of abundance. The elk's head represents wildlife. The motto is in Latin on the ribbon above the elk's head.

1805   Explored by Lewis and Clark for the United States
1860   Permanently settled by Mormons
1890   Admitted to the Union as the 43rd state

Capital—Boise

Lewis and Clark blazed a trail through Idaho in 1805, followed by English and American fur traders. Pioneers followed the Oregon Trail through southeast Idaho, although the first real settlement was established by a group of Mormons in 1860. The state was formed from the Idaho Territory, organized in 1863 when it separated from the Washington Territory.

ILLINOIS

Land of Lincoln

ILLINOIS

The Illinois state flag has a white field bordered in gold. The bald eagle, representing the United States, holds in its beak a streamer inscribed with the state motto. In the eagle's claws is a shield with thirteen bars and thirteen stars, representing the first thirteen states. The ground around the boulder symbolizes the rich prairie soil of Illinois.

1673 Explored by Louis Jolliet and Jacques Marquette for France
1720 Permanently settled by France
1818 Admitted to the Union as the 21st state

Capital—Springfield

The first permanent French settlement in this area was established in 1720 at Kaskaskia, in the province of Louisiana. After the French and Indian War, the region was ceded to the English. During the American Revolution, George Rogers Clark secured the area for the United States, and it became a part of the Northwest Territory in 1787. From 1800 to 1809 it was a part of the Indiana Territory. In 1809, the Illinois Territory was organized and statehood was granted in 1818.

INDIANA

Cross Roads of America

The Indiana state flag has two circles of gold stars around a burning torch, centered in a deep blue field. The outer circle of 13 stars stands for the 13 original states; the five stars in the lower inner circle represent the next five states to enter the Union; the large star above the flame symbolizes Indiana, and the torch stands for liberty and enlightenment.

1679 Explored by La Salle for France
1733 Permanently settled by the French
1816 Admitted to the Union as the 19th state

Capital—Indianapolis

In the early 18th century, French occupation of the area began with the construction of three forts: Miami, Ouiatenon, and Vincennes. Vincennes, built in 1732, was the only one to develop into a permanent settlement. France ceded the area to England after the French and Indian War, and following the American Revolution, the area became a part of the Northwest Territory.

17

IOWA

The Hawkeye State

The Iowa state flag bears the tricolor of France, representing the early French explorers. The white stripe represents the unwritten pages of Iowa's history. On that stripe a flying eagle carries in its beak a blue streamer with the state motto. The word "Iowa" is in red letters below the streamer.

1673 Explored by Louis Jolliet and Jacques Marquette for France
1788 Permanently settled by a French miner, Julien Dubuque
1846 Admitted to the Union as the 29th state

Capital—Des Moines

This area was a part of the Louisiana Purchase. Explored by Lewis and Clark in 1804, and Zebulon Pike in 1805, Iowa was included in the boundaries of several other territories before being separated in 1838. Numerous border disputes delayed the granting of statehood until 1846.

18

KANSAS

The Sunflower State

The Kansas state flag carries the state seal in the center of a blue flag. The state flower, the sunflower, is above the seal, and the name of the state is below in gold letters. The seal reflects the early pioneering days. Covered wagons are moving west, passing a farmer plowing his field. A steamboat is sailing on the Kansas river and Indians are hunting buffalo. The thirty-four stars mean that Kansas was the thirty-fourth state to join the Union.

1541   Explored by Francisco Vasquez de Coronado for Spain
1827   Permanently settled by the United States
1861   Admitted to the Union as the 34th state

Capital—Topeka

Kansas was a part of the Louisiana Purchase. The territory was originally used as reserved land for displaced eastern Indians. A battleground for pro- and anti-slavery groups, the state was formed from the Kansas Territory, organized in 1854 as part of the Kansas-Nebraska Act.

KENTUCKY

The Blue Grass State

The Kentucky state flag has the state seal in the center of a navy blue field. The two friends shaking hands are a reflection of the state motto "United We Stand, Divided We Fall." Kentucky is one of the four states that are a commonwealth instead of a state (along with Massachusetts, Pennsylvania, and Virginia). The state flower, goldenrod is also on the flag.

1673 Explored by Gabriel Arthur for England
1774 Permanently settled by American hunters and trappers
1792 Admitted to the Union as the 15th state

Capital—Frankfort

Following initial exploration in 1673, further attempts were not made again until Dr. Thomas Walker went to the area in 1750. He was followed in 1751 by Christopher Gist. In 1767, hunters, including Daniel Boone, moved into the territory, and land companies began to survey the area. By 1775, much of the territory was sold by the Cherokee Indians, and settlements arose at Harrodsburg and Boonesboro. In 1776, Kentucky was incorporated as a county of Virginia.

LOUISIANA

The Bayou State

The Louisiana state flag has a pelican feeding its young, in the center of a blue field. A symbol of Louisiana since the 1800s, the early settlers believed that the pelican was a generous and nurturing bird. The state motto appears on a white streamer beneath the pelican.

1528 Explored by Cabeza de Vaca for Spain
1699 Permanently settled by the French
1812 Admitted to the Union as the 18th state

Capital—Baton Rouge

This area was explored and claimed for France in 1682 by La Salle, whose attempt at establishing a colony five years later ended in his death. In 1698, Pierre Lemoyne built two forts along the Mississippi River. In 1711, Louisiana became a separate French colony, and in 1718 New Orleans was founded. Later, France ceded the territory to Spain, who gave it back to the French in 1800. In 1803, the territory was sold to the United States as part of the Louisiana Purchase.

21

MAINE

The Pine Tree State

The Maine state flag carries the state coat of arms on a blue field, of the same shade as the blue in the United States flag. The star represents the north star, which is what people have used since ancient times as a navigational aid. The seal shows a farmer and a seaman which represent the early settlers of the state. There is also a picture of a moose under a tall pine tree.

1000 Explored by Norsemen
1625 Permanently settled by the English
1820 Admitted to the Union as the 23rd state

Capital—Augusta

John Cabot probably explored Maine for the English in 1498, but Verrazano was the first to definitely explore the area, possibly as early as 1524, for France. In 1622 the region was under the control of the Plymouth Company. By the late 17th century, Massachusetts controlled Maine. They were separated in 1819, and statehood was granted in 1820 as a part of the Missouri Compromise.

MARYLAND

The Free State

The Maryland state flag bears the arms, or design, shown on the shield in the state seal. The black and gold colors and design represent the family of the Lords Baltimore, the Calverts. The red and white colors and design represent the Crossland family, the family name of the first Lord Baltimore's mother.

One of the thirteen original colonies
1608 Explored by Captain John Smith for England
1634 Permanently settled by the English
1788 Admitted to the Union as the 7th state

Capital—Annapolis

In 1632, King Charles I of England granted the territory now comprising the states of Maryland and Delaware to George Calvert, Lord Baltimore. At his death, his son succeeded to the title and organized a colonial expedition. Settlers arrived in Maryland in 1634, bought an existing Indian village, and named it Saint Mary's. The colony was founded on the principle of religious toleration.

MASSACHUSETTS

The Bay State

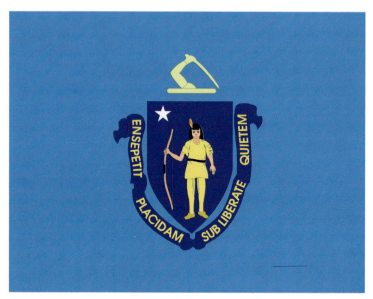

The Massachusetts state flag is white, with a shield on both sides. The white star represents Massachusetts as one of the original thirteen states. On one side, the shield depicts a native American in a stance of peace. The reverse side shows a pine tree on the shield.

One of the thirteen original colonies
1602 Explored by Bartholomew Gosnold for England
1620 Permanently settled by the English
1788 Admitted to the Union as the 6th state

Capital—Boston

A group of zealous Puritans known as Separatists or "Pilgrims" left England and established a colony at Plymouth in New England in 1620. In 1628, a Puritan settlement was started at Salem, called the Massachusetts Bay Colony. John Winthrop was elected governor in 1629 and Boston was founded in 1630. In 1692, under King William and Queen Mary, the Plymouth and Massachusetts Bay Colonies were consolidated and granted a new charter.

24

MICHIGAN

The Wolverine State

The Michigan state flag carries the state coat of arms in the center of a deep blue field. There is a man standing on a peninsula with his right hand raised in peace, and a gun in his left hand meaning "I will defend." The eagle stands for the United States, and the elk and moose represent Michigan.

Circa **1610**   Explored by the French
1668   Settled by Jacques Marquette for France
1837   Admitted to the Union as the 26th state

Capital—Lansing

Although settled by French missionaries and fur traders, the area came under British control after the French and Indian War. When the United States took charge after the American Revolution, Michigan was part of the Northwest Territory, even though the British were not driven out until 1795. In 1805, a separate Michigan Territory was created, and was gradually enlarged by the cession of Indian lands to the United States.

MINNESOTA

The North Star State

The large star on the state seal represents the north star; the 19 smaller stars show that Minnesota was the 19th state to join the Union after the original 13. The admission date, 1858, appears along with 1819, the date of settlement, and 1893, when the flag was adopted. A settler plows his field, an Indian rides into the sunset, and the stump with an embedded ax and the pine trees represent lumbering and the state tree. The state flower frames the seal.

1659   Explored by Pierre Esprit Radisson for France
1805   Permanently settled by American fur traders
1858   Admitted to the Union as the 32nd state

Capital—St. Paul

Fur traders worked in the region until France ceded it to England after the French and Indian War. Acquired by the United States after the American Revolution, the British maintained a stronghold in the territory until after the War of 1812. Treaties with the Sioux and Chippewa Indians opened the way for American settlement. The state was formed from the 1849 Minnesota Territory.

MISSISSIPPI

The Magnolia State

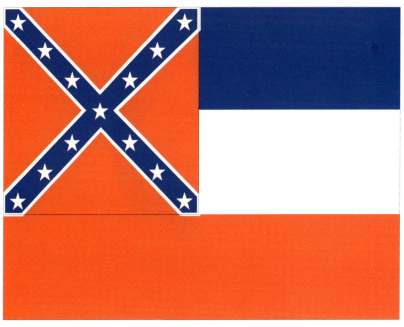

The Mississippi state flag has a square of red in the upper left corner, with 13 white stars on a cross of blue. The stars stand for the original 13 states. The field has three horizontal bands- blue, white, and red.

1540 Explored by Hernando de Soto for Spain
1699 Permanently settled by the French
1817 Admitted to the Union as the 20th state

Capital—Jackson

The first permanent settlement in this area was established at present day Biloxi. After the French and Indian War, the territory was ceded by the French to the English, who in turn surrendered it to Spain following the American Revolution. In 1795, Spain ceded most of Mississippi to the United States, and three years later, Mississippi was organized as a territory.

MISSOURI

The Show Me State

In the center of the flag is the seal of Missouri. It carries 24 stars, because it was the 24th state to join the Union. The circular seal in the center is in two parts - the right half is from the great seal of the United States; the left contains a moon representing Missouri as a new state, and a bear symbolizing courage. In the center ring is the motto "United We Stand, Divided We Fall." The Roman numerals give the date of the first state constitution in 1820.

1673 Explored by Louis Jolliet and Jacques Marquette for France
1735 Permanently settled by the French
1821 Admitted to the Union as the 24th state

Capital—Jefferson City

In 1764, France ceded the Louisiana territory to Spain, who ceded it back in 1800. France sold the region to the United States in 1803. In 1812 the region became the Missouri Territory. As a part of the Missouri Compromise, Missouri was admitted to the Union as a slave state.

28

MONTANA

The Big Sky Country

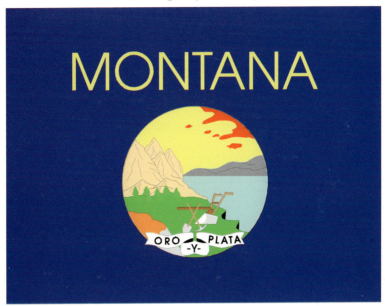

The Montana state flag has the state seal in the center of a blue field. The name Montana is above in large gold letters. The seal shows some of the state's beautiful scenery and reflects its early pioneer activity. The state motto at the bottom of the seal means "gold and silver" in Spanish, for Montana is also called "The Treasure State."

1742 Explored by the Verendrye brothers for France
1847 Permanently settled by Americans
1889 Admitted to the Union as the 41st state

Capital—Helena

Fur trappers worked in the region as early as the 1740s. Acquired as a portion of the Louisiana Purchase in 1803, Lewis and Clark explored the area in 1805. The region offered American fur traders a profitable business and was the scene of General Custer's defeat by the Sioux and Cheyenne Indians at Little Big Horn in 1876. The state was formed from the Montana Territory, created in 1864.

NEBRASKA

Tree Planter State

The Nebraska state flag carries the state seal, colored in silver and gold, in the center of a field of national blue. It depicts a blacksmith, wheat stands and a settler's cabin, as well as the transcontinental railroad, which was built westward from Omaha, beginning in 1865. The state motto and date of admission to the Union is also on the flag.

1682 Claimed by La Salle for France
1819 Settled by American military
1867 Admitted to the Union as the 37th state

Capital—Lincoln

France controlled the territory from 1700 to 1763, when the region was ceded to Spain. The area was sold to the United States in 1803, and was explored by Lewis and Clark soon afterward. Trails through Nebraska to the West led to the gradual settlement of the region. The state was formed from the Nebraska Territory, created in 1854. Nebraska is the only state with a unicameral legislature.

NEVADA

The Sage Brush State

The Nevada state flag has a field of solid cobalt blue. In the upper left corner are two sprays of sagebrush, formed in a half-wreath. The fivepointed star has "Nevada" spelled out between the points. The words "Battle Born" signifies Nevada's entry into the Union during the Civil War.

1775 Explored by Francisco Garces (Franciscan friar) for Spain
1849 Permanently settled by the United States
1864 Admitted to the Union as the 36th state

Capital—Carson City

Claimed by Mexico and ceded to the United States in 1848 after the Mexican War, Nevada was originally included as part of the Utah Territory created in 1850. Rapid settlement occurred after the discovery of the Comstock silver lode in 1859. The state was formed from the 1861 Nevada Territory.

NEW HAMPSHIRE

The Granite State

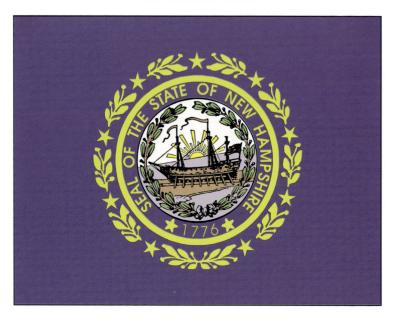

The New Hampshire state flag carries the state seal, surrounded by a golden laurel wreath with nine stars, in the center of a blue field. The stars signify that New Hampshire was the ninth state to ratify the Constitution of the United States. The date 1776 signifies the Declaration of Independence.

One of the thirteen original colonies
1605 Explored by Samuel de Champlain for France
1622 Permanently settled by the English
1788 Admitted to the Union as the 9th state

Capital—Concord

While the French were the first to explore in this area, it was John Smith's explorations, maps, and reports of the region which led to its eventual settlement. In 1622, John Mason and Sir Ferdinando Gorges received a land grant and founded settlements at Dover and Portsmouth. Others followed, but by 1643, all had joined the Massachusetts Bay Colony. In 1680, New Hampshire became a separate royal province.

32

NEW JERSEY

The Garden State

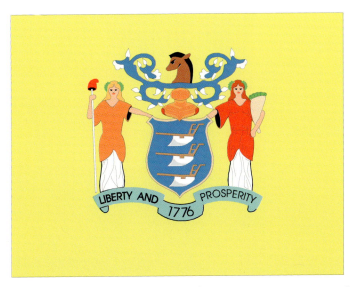

The New Jersey state flag is buff-color, with the state seal emblazoned in the center. The colors, chosen by George Washington, were used by the New Jersey troops during the Revolutionary War. The horse on the shield is the state animal, and the helmet shows that New Jersey governs itself. The two goddesses represent the motto. The blue shield with three plows symbolizes the "Garden State," and the date 1776 refers to the Revolution.

One of the thirteen original colonies
1524 Explored by Giovanni da Verrazano for France
1664 Permanently settled by the English
1787 Admitted to the Union as the 3rd state

Capital—Trenton

Dutch merchants set up trading posts at present day Jersey City in 1618 and Fort Nassau in 1624. The Swedes were forced out in 1655. Eventually, the Dutch surrendered control to the English. Lord John Berkeley and Sir George Carteret were granted the region, which was divided into East and West Jersey in 1676. The two colonies were united in 1702 as a royal colony.

NEW MEXICO

The Cactus State

Red and yellow, the colors of Ferdinand and Isabella of Spain, were carried by Coronado in 1540. The flag's center motif is the ancient symbol of the Native American people of Zia. The four sets of four rays represent the four gifts: the four directions, the four seasons, the day (sunrise, noon, evening, and night), and the life cycle (childhood, youth, middle years and old age). All of these are bound together in a circle of love, which is without beginning or end.

1539 Explored by Marcos de Niza for Spain
1598 Permanently settled by Spanish missionaries
1912 Admitted to the Union as the 47th state

Capital—Santa Fe

The region was controlled by the Spanish until Mexico won its independence in 1821. Most of New Mexico was acquired by the United States at the end of the Mexican War in 1848. In 1853, the United States bought the land which forms the present boundary with Mexico in the Gadsden Purchase. The state was formed from the New Mexico Territory, created in 1850.

34

NEW YORK

The Empire State

The flag carries the state coat of arms, appearing in the center of a dark blue field. It depicts the badge of the Duke of York, with the sun and an American Bald Eagle perched on the new world. On the left is Liberty; at her feet is a crown symbolizing freedom from England. On the right, Liberty wears a blindfold with a sword in her right hand and scales in her left hand, signifying equality under the law.

One of the thirteen original colonies
1609   Explored by Henry Hudson for the Dutch
1624   Permanently settled by the Dutch
1788   Admitted to the Union as the 11th state

Capital—Albany

French explorer Samuel de Champlain and English explorer Henry Hudson (for the Dutch) investigated this portion of the New World in 1609. By the 1620s the Dutch had established a permanent settlement which they named New Amsterdam. In 1664, they surrendered control of New Amsterdam to the English. The territory was renamed New York after James, Duke of York and Albany, who later became King James II.

NORTH CAROLINA

The Tarheel State

The red, white and blue are a tribute to the American flag. The initials "NC" and a star designate it as one of the original 13 states. May 20, 1775, refers to the Mecklenburg Declaration of Independence. April 12, 1776, is the date the Halifax Resolves was written, authorizing the state's delegates at the Continental Congress to sign the Declaration of Independence.

One of the thirteen original colonies
1524 Explored by Giovanni da Verrazano for France
1650 Permanently settled by the English
1789 Admitted to the Union as the 12th state

Capital—Raleigh

Queen Elizabeth I of England granted Sir Walter Raleigh the right to establish a colony in 1584. Two settlements at Roanoke Island (1585, 1587) were unsuccessful. By 1650, only a few colonists from Virginia had settled in the region. In 1663, the Carolinas became a proprietary colony, divided into North and South Carolina, with grants given to eight proprietors by King Charles II. North Carolina became a royal colony in 1729.

NORTH DAKOTA

The Sioux State

The North Dakota state flag has a field of blue, with the national emblem in the center. It shows a bald eagle with an olive branch (for peace) in its right claw, and arrows (for power) in its left claw. The national motto is on a streamer in the eagle's beak. Above its head are 13 stars for the original 13 states, and sun rays depict the rising of America. On the eagle's breast is a shield with thirteen stripes, and below the eagle, "North Dakota" appears on a red scroll.

1738 Explored by La Verendrye for France
1797 Permanently settled by British fur traders
1889 Admitted to the Union as the 39th state

Capital—Bismarck

Included in the Louisiana Purchase, the area was sold to the United States in 1803. Lewis and Clark explored the region in 1804 as an important trade route to the Northwest. For many years, the area was only inhabited by Indians and fur trappers. The state was formed from the Dakota Territory, organized in 1861.

OHIO

The Buckeye State

Ohio's flag is pennant-shaped, similar to the cavalry guidon carried during the Civil War. It has a field of horizontal stripes, three red and two white. The blue triangle has 17 white stars, which indicate that it was the 17th state to join the Union. The large O suggests the first letter in Ohio and the Northwest Territory. The red disc symbolizes the buckeye seed from the state tree.

1669   Explored by La Salle for France
1788   Permanently settled by American fur traders
1803   Admitted to the Union as the 17th state

Capital—Columbus

In the late 17th and early 18th centuries, French and English traders competed and clashed in the region. Following the French and Indian War, in 1763, the land was ceded to the English. The United States acquired the area following the American Revolution. Ohio was included in the Northwest Territory, created in 1787, and became a state in 1803.

OKLAHOMA

The Sooner State

The state flag honors the sixty different groups of Native Americans living in Oklahoma. The blue field comes from a flag carried by Choctaw soldiers during the Civil War. The shield in the center is an Osage warrior battle shield, made of buffalo hide and decorated with eagle feathers. Two symbols of peace rest on the shield - the calumet or peace pipe and the olive branch. The crosses on the shield are Native American signs for stars.

1541 Explored by Francisco Vasquez de Coronado for Spain
1889 Permanently settled by American homesteaders
1907 Admitted to the Union as the 46th state

Capital—Oklahoma City

Though claimed by the Spanish and French, the region remained inhabited primarily by Indians. In 1803 the United States bought the area in the Louisiana Purchase, and it became a part of the Missouri and Arkansas Territories. First set aside as a new homeland for displaced eastern Indians of the Five Civilized Tribes, Oklahoma was opened to homesteaders in 1889. The state was formed from the Oklahoma Territory, organized in 1890.

OREGON

The Beaver State

The Oregon state flag displays the state seal in gold in the center of a navy-blue field. The seal depicts the sun over the Pacific, mountains, forests, and a covered wagon. The name of the state appears above the seal, and below is the year of statehood. A beaver in gold appears on the reverse side of the flag.

1543 Explored by Bartolome Ferrelo for Spain
1811 Permanently settled by fur traders
1859 Admitted to the Union as the 33rd state

Capital—Salem

The first American settlers entered the area in 1834 and continued to arrive via the Oregon Trail into the Willamette Valley throughout the 1840s. Disputed claims to the region with the British were settled by 1846. The state was formed from the 1848 Oregon Territory.

PENNSYLVANIA

Keystone State

The design is the state coat of arms. The eagle atop the shield represents the United States, with an olive branch and a stalk of corn crossed at the bottom. The shield is supported by rearing black horses. The ship represents Pennsylvania's trade. The plow and sheaves of wheat symbolize wealth from abundant harvests, as well as wealth from human thought and action. The state motto is on a red banner below the shield.

One of the thirteen original colonies
1615 Explored by Cornelius Hendricksen for the Dutch
1643 Permanently settled by the Swedes
1787 Admitted to the Union as the 2nd state

Capital—Harrisburg

The Swedes first settled the region of the Delaware River and held it until the Dutch claimed the territory in 1655. The English gained control in 1664, and in 1681, Charles II granted most of Pennsylvania to William Penn. Because of its guarantee of religious freedom, the colony, which began in 1682, drew many immigrants.

RHODE ISLAND

The Ocean State

*The Rhode Island state flag is white, sometimes edged with a
yellow fringe. In the center is a gold anchor with the state
motto inscribed on a blue banner beneath it. Thirteen gold
stars, representing the original colonies, surround the anchor
and motto.*

One of the thirteen original colonies
1511 Possibly explored by Miguel de Corte-Real for Portugal
1636 Permanently settled by the English
1790 Admitted to the Union as the 13th state

Capital—Providence

Roger Williams established the first settlement at Providence
in 1636. Portsmouth and Newport were founded in 1638 and
1639. In 1643, Warwick was established by Samuel Gorton
and a charter was obtained for Providence, Portsmouth, and
Newport. In 1647, all four settlements united. King Charles
II granted the unified colony a charter in 1663.

42

SOUTH CAROLINA

Palmetto State

Among the oldest flag designs still in use, it dates to 1765 when three white crescents were used on a blue flag to protest the Stamp Act. Colonel William Moultrie later designed a flag for South Carolina soldiers using the blue color of their uniforms as the field and the silver crescent from their caps. The Palmetto tree was added after the battle on Sullivan's Island in 1776.

One of the thirteen original colonies
1521 Explored by the Spanish
1670 Permanently settled by the English
1788 Admitted to the Union as the 8th state

Capital—Columbia

After exploring in 1521, the Spanish attempted a settlement in 1526, but it was shortly abandoned. A group of French Huguenots established a colony on Parris Island in 1562 which lasted about a year. In 1566, the Spanish attempted a fortified settlement on Parris Island, which lasted until 1586. Claimed by England in 1663, the Carolinas were granted to a group of eight proprietors, and a colony was established to the south in 1670. In 1729, South Carolina became a royal colony.

SOUTH DAKOTA

Mount Rushmore State

The South Dakota flag pictures the state seal, encircled by a serrated sun, or sunburst. It depicts farming, cattle ranching, mining, manufacturing and lumbering. The Missouri River is pictured with the Black Hills in the distance. The steam boat represents transportation and trade.

1743 Explored by the Verendrye brothers for France
1817 Permanently settled by American fur traders
1889 Admitted to the Union as the 40th state

Capital—Pierre

The Dakotas became a part of the United States as a result of the Louisiana Purchase in 1803. Fur traders moved into the area following the Lewis and Clark expedition in 1804. The state was formed from the 1861 Dakota Territory, which grew in population with the discovery of gold in the Black Hills in 1874.

44

TENNESSEE

The Volunteer State

The Tennessee state flag has a red field bordered by a white and blue stripe. The state's three sections—east, middle, and west— are represented by three white stars within a blue circle bordered in white. The stars also signify that Tennessee was the third state to enter the Union after the thirteen original states.

1540 Explored by Hernando de Soto for Spain
1769 Permanently settled by the English
1796 Admitted to the Union as the 16th state

Capital—Nashville

Charles II of England included this territory in the Carolina grants made in 1663 and 1665. In 1673, Englishmen James Needham and Gabriel Arthur explored the region and visited Cherokee and Chickasaw Indian villages. During the French and Indian War, pioneers moved into the area, and Daniel Boone blazed a trail over the mountains in 1775. Tennessee was organized as a separate territory in 1790.

TEXAS

Lone Star State

The single or lone star is derived from the flag that flew over Texas from 1836 to 1839. It was under this flag that the people of Texas fought the revolution against Mexico. Texas won the war, declared its independence in 1836 and became the Republic of Texas. It remained an independent country until it joined the United States in 1845. The color blue stands for loyalty, white for purity and red for bravery.

1519 Explored by de Pineda for Spain
1682 Permanently settled by Spanish missionaries
1845 Admitted to the Union as the 28th state

Capital—Austin

Spain controlled the region until 1821 when Mexico gained its independence. At that time, the United States reached agreement with Mexico allowing Americans to colonize the territory. Conflicts between settlers and the Mexican government led to a revolution in 1835. In 1836, Texas won its independence and remained a separate republic until its admission as a state.

UTAH

Beehive State

Two dates appear on the state seal: one commemorates the original settlement in 1847 and the other the admission into the Union in 1896. The beehive is the symbol of industry. The sego lily stands for peace. The national flags show that Utah supports the United States. The eagle is also a national emblem, standing for protection in peace and war.

1776 Explored by Silvestre Velez de Escalante and Francisco Atanasio Dominguez for Spain
1847 Permanently settled by American Mormons
1896 Admitted to the Union as the 45th state

Capital—Salt Lake City

Although the area was first explored by the Spanish, English and American fur traders soon entered the region. Mass migrations of Mormons from eastern states occurred in the 1840s. In 1848, the territory was ceded to the United States after the Mexican War. In 1849, the Mormons created the State of Deseret, but it was denied admission to the United States. Utah was formed from the Territory of Utah, organized by the United States in 1850.

VERMONT

Green Mountain State

The Vermont state coat of arms appears in the center of a blue field, and includes a shield bearing a Vermont landscape. Crossed pine branches surround the lower part of the shield, with the motto on a red scroll beneath it. Above is a buck's head, representing Vermont's wildlife.

1609 Explored by Samuel de Champlain for France
1724 Permanently settled by the English
1791 Admitted to the Union as the 14th state

Capital—Montpelier

Colonists from Massachusetts established the first permanent settlement in 1724. Following a dispute over this territory between New Hampshire and New York, George III granted it to New York. Under the leadership of Ethan Allen, New Hampshire settlers rebelled. In 1777, Vermont seceded from New York and became an independent republic, until its admission to the Union in 1791. Vermont's constitution of 1777 was the first to provide for universal suffrage and the prohibition of slavery.

48

VIRGINIA

Old Dominion State

The seal on Virginia's deep blue flag portrays the state motto "Sic Semper Tryannis" or "Thus Ever to Tyrants." The woman, virtue, represents Virginia. The man holds a whip and chain, symbolizing tyranny. They have fought a battle, and the tyrant lies on the ground defeated, his fallen crown nearby.

The first permanent English settlement in North America and the first of the thirteen original colonies.

1570   Spanish mission established near the York River
1607   Permanently settled by the English at Jamestown
1788   Admitted to the Union as the 10th state

Capital—Richmond

A permanent settlement was established by the Virginia Company of London in 1607 under its original charter. In 1609, James I granted a second charter, which increased Virginia's territory to its maximum size, stretching from the Atlantic to the Pacific Oceans. Following the American Revolution, Virginia relinquished her northern and western territories, which eventually were divided into individual states.

WASHINGTON

Evergreen State

George Washington is pictured on the state flag along with the date the state was admitted into the Union. The only state to use a green background on its flag, the color represents the rich forest land of Washington.

1579 Coastal areas explored by Sir Francis Drake for England
1810 Permanently settled by British fur traders
1889 Admitted to the Union as the 42nd state

Capital—Olympia

Lewis and Clark opened the area for American activity in their 1805 explorations. In 1818, British and Americans agreed to joint occupation of the area. Because of conflicts, however, a treaty was necessary in 1846 which established a boundary between the United States and Canada. The state was formed from the Washington Territory, organized in 1853.

WEST VIRGINIA

The Mountain State

The West Virginia state flag displays the state seal in the center of a white flag, bordered in blue. Founded during the Civil War, the date June 20, 1863, on the rock, commemorates its statehood. Two men represent farming and mining, and two rifles with liberty caps symbolize the people's readiness to defend their freedom. Around the shield are wreaths of rhododendron, the state flower.

1671 Explored by Thomas Batts and Robert Fallam for England
1727 Permanently settled by the English
1863 Admitted to the Union as the 35th state

Capital—Charleston

A part of the original colony of Virginia, conflicts arose between western Virginians and those in the east after the American Revolution, particularly concerning the issue of slavery. When Virginia seceded from the Union in 1861, pro-Union westerners met at Wheeling, formed a government, and applied for admission to the Union as a separate state.

WISCONSIN

The Badger State

The Wisconsin state flag has the main design of the state seal centered on a dark blue field. In the center of the shield is the shield of the United States and its motto. The surrounding pictures represent the state's main industries, mining, shipping, labor and agriculture. The cornucopia and pile of lead stand for farm products and minerals that help bring prosperity.

1634 Explored by Jean Nicolet for France
1764 Permanently settled by the English
1848 Admitted to the Union as the 30th state

Capital—Madison

As a result of the French and Indian War, French supremacy in Wisconsin ended with the occupation of the region by the British in 1760. The area was ceded to the United States after the American Revolution, and became a part of the Northwest Territory. The opening of lead mines and the influx of settlers led to hostilities between whites and Indians and the resulting Black Hawk War of 1832. The state was formed from the 1836 Wisconsin Territory.

WYOMING

Equality State or The Cowboy State

*The flag carries the state seal upon a white silhouette of a bison.
The men represent cattle ranching and mining. The dates 1869
and 1890 tell when Wyoming organized its first government as
a territory of the United States and when it became a state. The
white border stands for purity and the red border for the blood
of early pioneers and the original Indian population.*

1807 Explored by John Colter for the United States
1834 Permanently settled by American fur traders
1890 Admitted to the Union as the 44th state

Capital—Cheyenne

Wyoming was home to more than a dozen Indian tribes when
the first American traders entered the area. The region was
acquired in portions by the United States: the east in the
Louisiana Purchase, 1803; the south in the Texas annexation,
1845; the west in the Oregon Boundary Settlement, 1846; and
the southwest with Mexican cession of the area in 1848. The
state was formed from the Wyoming Territory, organized in
1868. It was the first state to give women the vote.

Alabama—joined Union in 1819 as 22nd state

Alaska—joined Union in 1959 as 49th state

Arizona—joined Union in 1912 as 48th state

Arkansas—joined Union in 1836 as 25th state

California—joined Union in 1850 as 31st state

Colorado—joined Union in 1876 as 38th state

Connecticut—one of the 13 original colonies, the 5th state to ratify the Constitution on January 9, 1788

Delaware—one of the 13 original colonies, the 1st state to ratify the Constitution on December 7, 1787

Florida—joined Union in 1845 as 27th state

Georgia—one of the 13 original colonies, the 4th state to ratify the Constitution on January 2, 1788

Hawaii—joined Union in 1959 as 50th state

Idaho—joined Union in 1890 as 43rd state

Illinois—joined Union in 1818 as 21st state

Indiana—joined Union in 1816 as 19th state

Iowa—joined Union in 1846 as 29th state

Kansas—joined Union in 1861 as 34th state

Kentucky—joined Union in 1792 as 15th state

Louisiana—joined Union in 1812 as 18th state

Maine—joined the Union in 1820 as 23rd state

Maryland—one of the 13 original colonies, the 7th state to ratify the Constitution on April 28, 1788

Massachusetts—one of the 13 original colonies, the 6th state to ratify the Constitution on February 6, 1788

Michigan—joined Union in 1837 as 26th state

Minnesota—joined Union in 1858 as 32nd state

Mississippi—joined Union in 1817 as 20th state

Missouri—joined Union in 1821 as 24th state

Montana—joined Union in 1889 as 41st state

Nebraska—joined Union in 1867 as 37th state

Nevada—joined Union in 1864 as 36th state

New Hampshire—one of the 13 original colonies, the 9th state to ratify the Constitution on June 21, 1788

New Jersey—one of the 13 original colonies, the 3rd state to ratify the Constitution on December 18, 1787

New Mexico—joined Union in 1912 as 47th state

New York—one of the 13 original colonies, the 11th state to ratify the Constitution on July 26, 1788

North Carolina—one of the 13 original colonies, the 12th state to ratify the Constitution on November 21, 1789

North Dakota—joined Union in 1889 as 39th state

Ohio—joined Union in1803 as 17th state

Oklahoma—joined Union in 1907 as 46th state

Oregon—joined Union in 1859 as 33rd state

Pennsylvania—one of the 13 original colonies, the 2nd state to ratify the Constitution on December 12, 1787

Rhode Island—one of the 13 original colonies, the 13th state to ratify the Constitution on May 29, 1790

South Carolina—one of the 13 original colonies, the 8th state to ratify the Constitution on May 23, 1788

South Dakota—joined Union in 1889 as 40th state

Tennessee—joined Union in 1796 as 16th state

Texas—joined Union in 1845 as 28th state

Utah—joined Union in 1896 as 45th state

Vermont—joined Union in 1791 as 14th state

Virginia—one of the 13 original colonies, the 10th state to ratify the Constitution on June 25, 1788

Washington—joined Union in 1889 as 42nd state

West Virginia—joined Union in 1863 as 35th state

Wisconsin—joined Union in 1846 as 30th state

Wyoming—joined Union in 1890 as 44th state

THE THIRTEEN ORIGINAL COLONIES

Connecticut—one of the 13 original colonies, first settled in 1634 by those seeking freedom from the harsh conditions in the Massachusetts Bay Colony, leader was Thomas Hooker, preacher

Delaware—one of the 13 original colonies, first settled in 1631 by the Dutch, the only state whose territory once belonged to Sweden

Georgia—one of the 13 original colonies, first settled in 1733 by James Oglethorpe

Maryland—one of the 13 original colonies, first settled in 1634 as a refuge for Catholics

Massachusetts—one of the 13 original colonies, first settled in 1620 by the Pilgrims at Plymouth

New Hampshire—one of the 13 original colonies, first settled in 1623

New Jersey—one of the 13 original colonies, first settled in 1638 by the Dutch, who established a settlement along the Delaware River

New York—one of the 13 original colonies, first settled in 1623 by the Dutch at Fort Orange

North Carolina—one of the 13 original colonies, first settled in 1585 by the English at Roanoke, the Lost Colony, 1st English child born in North America, Virginia Dare in 1587

Pennsylvania—one of the 13 original colonies, first settled in 1643

Rhode Island—one of the 13 original colonies, first settled in 1636 as a free haven for religious worship in America

South Carolina—one of the 13 original colonies, first settled by the English in 1670

Virginia—one of the 13 original colonies, first settled by the English in 1607 at Jamestown